49 Excuses for Skipping Gym Class

Copyright © 2015, 2022 by James Warwood

Published by Curious Squirrel Press

All rights reserved

No part of this book may be used, stored or reproduced in any manner whatsoever without written permission from the author or publisher.

Book cover design by: James Warwood
Book interior design by: Mala Letra / Lic. Sara F. Salomon

ISBN: 9798429205830
ebook ISBN: B0165M0ILI

THE EXCUSE ENCYCLOPEDIA

Book Five:
49 Excuses for Skipping Gym Class

James Warwood

BOOK FIVE

Excuses for Skipping Gym Class

GYM CLASS EXCUSES

1. THE DOCTORS NOTE EXCUSE

I've got a Doctor's Note for today lesson . . .

. . . turns out that sucking at sport is a newly discovered and extremely rare condition called *'Pretenditous'*. Unfortunately there is no known cure and as long as I have an active imagination I can't do Gym Class until I finish High School.

2. THE LEARN-BY-EXAMPLE EXCUSE

As a keen and dedicated gym student...

.... I feel I need a detailed demonstration of how to use every single piece of equipment in the school Gym. You can start with this one. I designed it myself.

3. THE BULKING-UP EXCUSE

Sorry Coach, but I am currently in the middle of a bulk-up session . . .

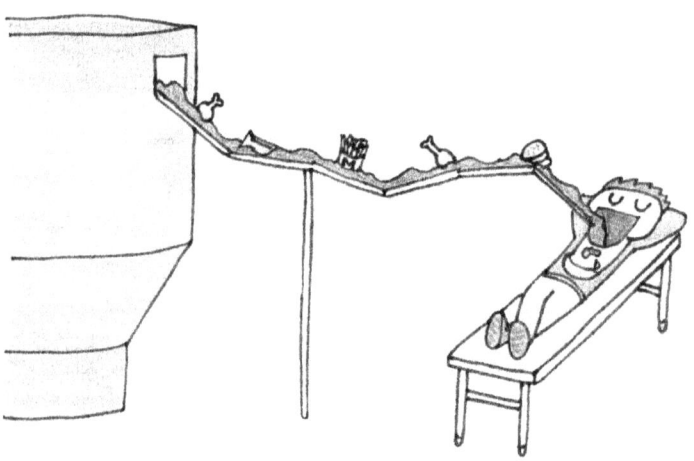

. . . as you can see this is an intense workout. Unfortunately I can not join in with the lesson until I have finished all this food, then slept for an hour, then completed another session I like to call *'the burp-a-thon'*.

4. THE SUBSTITUTE EXCUSE

To learn the values of sportsmanship I have brought along my own substitute...

... she is really good at running and catching so, if I were you Coach, I would play her outfield.

5. THE DEAD BALL EXCUSE

I have some terrible news, Coach. Spalding is dead . . .

. . . when we returned him to the cupboard yesterday he was fine. This morning we opened the door and found him like this. The whole class are devastated by this awful tragedy. See you in 6 months.

6. THE ROBOTS EXCUSE

Modern technology is moving closer and closer towards artificial intelligence and this school has also encouraged the pursuit of progress and achievement . . .

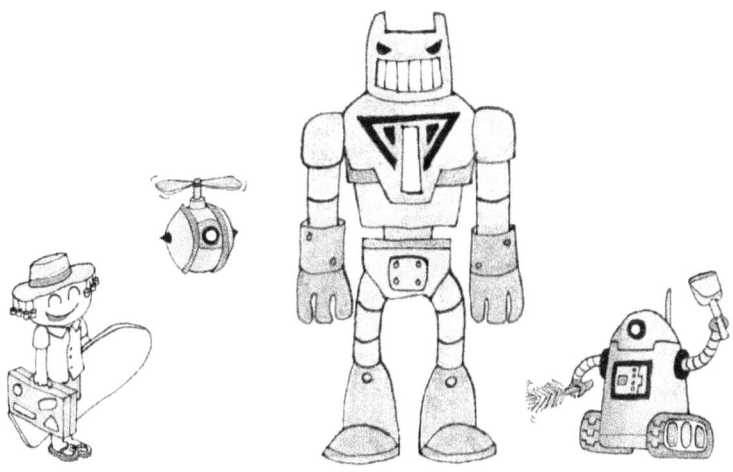

. . . here are my robots. The first one tells everyone what to do, the second crushes anyone who disobeys and the last one cleans up the mess. They will take over from here so I can do more important stuff.

7. THE SLEEP WALKING EXCUSE

I have already had my daily recommended amount of exercise...

... last night to be exact.

8. THE FITNESS PROGRAMME EXCUSE

Thanks to my new fitness programme I don't need to do Gym Class ever again . . .

. . . I simply turn my head to the left, then turn my head to the right, then back to the left again. I do this every time someone offers me a cookie.

9. THE MUSCULAR EXCUSE

I'm afraid I can not take part in Gym Class anymore...

... my muscles are completely full! If I lifted another weight my arms will explode.

10. THE SOCKS EXCUSE

My socks, they . . . they don't . . . they don't match . . .

. . . the ancient prophecy has come true. Run for your lives, save yourselves . . . THE APOCALYPSE IS COMING!

11. THE PRAYER EXCUSE

I'm trading in Gym Class for prayer . . .

. . . if this works it'll benefit everyone. You can thank me later.

12. THE NATURE EXCUSE

Look at these examples from nature . . .

THE GIANT TURTLE   THE BLUE WHALE   THE BUNNY RABBIT

. . . the Giant Turtle: sleeps for 16 hours a day and has a lifespan of 100 years. The Blue Whale: eats 4 tons of krill a day and has a lifespan of 80 years. The Bunny Rabbit: eats mainly grass or hay, can reach speeds of 18 miles an hour and has a lifespan of 3 years. It seems nature is telling me to eat, sleep and not exercise to live a long and happy life.

13. THE FLOWER EXCUSE

I have decided to trade in my legs for a stem . . .

. . . I'm now a flower that can only be watered with Lucozade. If you need me I will be in the planet pot next to the 52" Flat Screen TV in the Teachers Lounge.

14. THE ACCIDENT EXCUSE

I've had a terrible accident, Coach . . .

. . . I was practicing doing a forward roll when it happened. Looks like I will have to spend the rest of my life as a ball.

15. THE R.S.P.C.S. EXCUSE

I have started a new school society called the R.S.P.C.S. . . .

. . . it is our responsibility to protect and care for sport in its natural habitat. For far too long this school has exploited and enslaved sport by means of enforced labour and cruelty. It stops now. We say NO to sports slavery. Join my society and boycott Gym Class before endangered sports become extinct.

16. THE LOST PROPERTY EXCUSE

Listen, how about we make a deal . . .

. . . if you cancel Gym Class you can have anything from the lost property box and none of us will tell on you. And if you let us play on our phones I'll write a letter to the Headteacher explaining how I think you deserve a massive pay rise and a company sports car.

17. THE LETTER EXCUSE

I have a letter from my parents . . .

. . . it explains why I can not do Gym Class today. And if that doesn't work I have also got letters from the Queen of England and Arnold Schwarzenegger.

18. THE CONSPIRACY EXCUSE

Don't overreact, but I think the new Gym Teachers are killing off the weedy kids . . .

. . . why do I think they're murderers? How else can you explain the fact that there's only ever muscular kids at the Gym these days?

19. THE CHEWING EXCUSE

I realised something last night, I am really good at one exercise . . .

. . . chewing! Earlier in the year you told us - *'practice makes perfect'* - so I'll be over here training really really hard.

49 Excuses for Skipping Gym Class

20. THE VIDEO GAMER EXCUSE

Unfortunately I can't join in today . . .

. . . if I do 10 laps of the pitch then I won't have any energy left to play video games tonight. Sorry but I have got priorities to consider.

21. THE DEATH STAR EXCUSE

Good news Coach. I've been accepted into the *'Death Star Internship Programme'*...

... it was nice training with you all but becoming an Intergalactic Overlord in a giant circular spaceship is my destiny. Plus I've already checked and there is no Gym Class at Sith School.

22. THE NEW EXERCISES EXCUSE

I have developed some new exercises for the class to try...

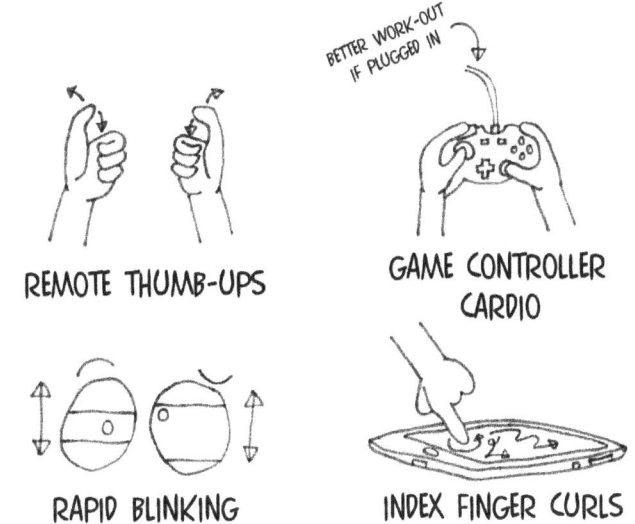

REMOTE THUMB-UPS

GAME CONTROLLER CARDIO (BETTER WORK-OUT IF PLUGGED IN)

RAPID BLINKING

INDEX FINGER CURLS

... the great thing about my revolutionary exercises is that you do all of them sitting down. In fact you don't even have to change into your gym kit. Amazing, I know.

23. THE PHONE CALL EXCUSE

I just got the most important phone call of my entire life . . .

. . . the President of the United States of America is on his way. Quickly, get into a line and salute while standing completely motionless like they do on TV. Otherwise the President might take offence and throw us all in jail.

24. THE FORTUNE TELLER EXCUSE

I was going to do Gym Class today . . .

. . . but my Fortune Teller advised me to stay away from all forms of exercise. Something about a *'foreboding accident'*, sounds painful doesn't it.

25. THE TOOTH EXCUSE

According to my dentist this tooth is dangerously close to falling out . . .

. . . and according to the Tooth Fairy if I lose a tooth while doing a roly-poly my tooth is void of all monetary value. Everyone knows she does not except any teeth that have travelled through the body's digestive system!

26. THE JIM EXCUSE

So it turns out I've been going to the Gym for months and months . . .

. . . the guy who always serves me at McDonalds is called Jim! I know, great isn't it. Maybe we should take the whole class to Jim now and have a workout at the fastfood joint.

27. THE HAND-STAND EXCUSE

Good news, I have mastered the hand-stand . . .

. . . took me all night to construct this masterpiece but just take a look at the beauty. Look how it balances my hand perfectly while I am in a standing position. It's so good I made one for my foot too.

28. THE PROTEIN SUPPLEMENT EXCUSE

This just arrived for me . . .

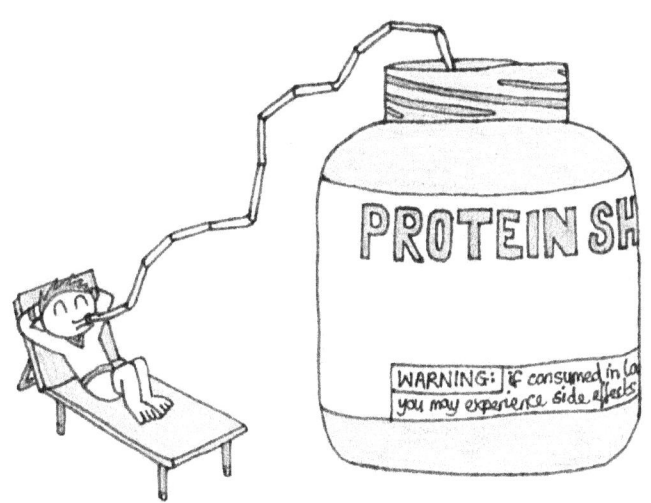

. . . so I don't need to do Gym Class today, I'll drink this instead.

29. THE BRIEFCASE EXCUSE

Oh dear. This isn't my gym kit . . .

. . . I must have picked up the wrong bag, but if anyone is interested I could do my Dad's presentation on the quarterly stats.

30. THE CHESTNUT EXCUSE

The new chestnut diet I have been trialling for Heat Magazine has been causing two very annoying problems . . .

. . . number 1. I smell like a giant chestnut, and number 2. this gang of squirrels keeps on trying to kidnap me and bury me underneath a tree for the winter months.

31. THE NEW SPORT EXCUSE

I have invented a new sport. I call it *'Xtreme Simon Says'*...

...it is exactly the same as normal *'Simon Says'* except it is just for Teachers and if you get it wrong Gretel from the senior Dodgeball Team will throw this ball at you. Ready, steady, GO!

32. THE EVIL PLOT EXCUSE

My plot to overthrow the school council is almost complete . . .

. . . I'm thinking of changing things up, you know, move away from democracy and try a dictatorship. So if you give me some time to finalise my plans I'll make you number 2. How does that sound?

33. THE ANTI-SPORT EXCUSE

Coach, I think there is something wrong with me . . .

. . . when I exercise my cheeks turn red, my armpits smell, my breathing doubles and my heartbeat triples. Surely the only possible explanation is that I am allergic to exercise.

34. THE FRIES EXCUSE

Pardon Coach, today in Gym Class we are going to *'do some exercise'* . . .

. . . I thought you said *'bring extra-fries'*. I spent a months worth of pocket money on all these fries and it is too late to take them back now. We can not let them go to waste now, can we?

35. THE POKEMON EXCUSE

I think I misunderstood what today's lesson is about...

... I thought you said *'we will be training up to battle the Gym Leader'*, instead of *'we will be training up on the gym equipment'*.

36. THE EMPTY BELLY EXCUSE

As you can see there is no food in my belly . . .

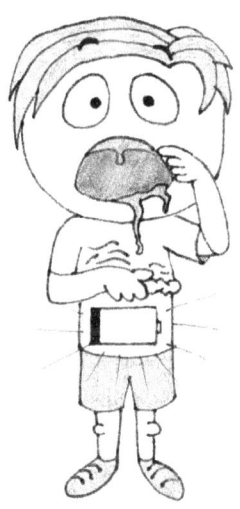

. . . I'm running dangerously low on power. How can you expect me, a growing lad, to do strenuous exercise without the proper energy source required?

37. THE TORNADO EXCUSE

Holy Moley! Tornado Doris just passed through the Gym Cupboard . . .

. . . don't go in there Coach, don't even poke your head in. The destruction to the gym equipment will be extremely upsetting to someone of your profession. I recommend that we all head to the local checkpoint, declare ourselves alive and take some time to mourn our destroyed-beyond-repair school equipment.

38. THE BRAIN EXCUSE

I understand that my body needs exercise . . .

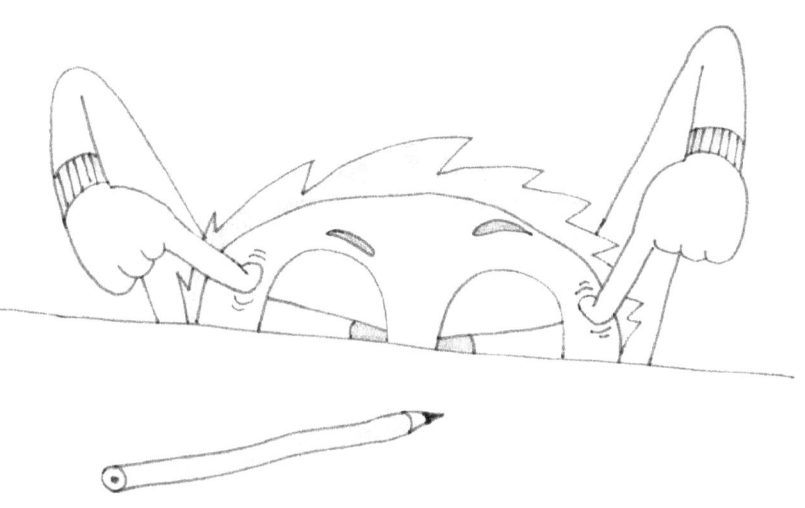

. . . but so does my brain, right? With this in mind I'll be doing some brain training instead of running laps today. If you need me I will be in the corner attempting to move this pencil with my mind.

39. THE DIGESTION EXCUSE

Sorry but I cannot do any strenuous exercise for the next two hours . . .

. . . I ate a large portion of chips for lunch and polished off the emergency chocolate bars you keep in the bottom draw in your office. Two hours is the recommended amount of nap-time required for healthy digestion so please try to keep the noise down Coach.

40. THE EXPERIMENT EXCUSE

We have been learning about the extraordinary metabolism of adult Gym Teachers in Science Class. So . . .

. . . I was wondering if you would run on this treadmill for two hours while I monitor your metabolism levels for my homework.

41. THE ONE RING EXCUSE

I was practising long jump when I landed on this ring . . .

. . . there's some funny-looking writing around the edge. So I guess that means I've got to go on a really really long journey and toss it in a volcano. Wish me luck!

42. THE RAIN DANCE EXCUSE

I found this costume in the cupboard Coach...

...then all of a sudden my ancestral instincts took over and I began dancing and chanting and jumping like a frog around this fire until it started to rain. Guess that means we can't do outdoor games, darn you unpredictable weather.

43. THE DEMON GYM TEACHER EXCUSE

I am the Demon Gym Teacher and I am here for Miss Jones . . .

. . . you have been summoned to stand trial for crimes against students. I recommend finding yourself a good lawyer as the jury down in Hell will be a tough crowd, they all hated Gym Class too.

44. THE PHOTO-BOMBER EXCUSE

Good news everyone. I've got a job as a professional Photo-Bomber...

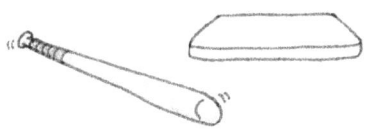

... I am on call 24/7. Oh, just got a call. A happy couple is about to take a selfie one mile east from here. See you later everyone, got a photo to ruin.

45. THE PAPER CUT EXCUSE

I've been looking forward to Gym Class all week but . . .

. . . unfortunately it happened again. Look, I've got a debilitating paper cut. It's 6mm deep and 8mm long this time. I think Art Class doesn't want me to exercise because this seems to happen every week.

46. THE FORGETFUL EXCUSE

Sorry Coach, I have forgotten my gym clothes . . .

. . . I must be having a forgetful day because I have also forgotten who poured petrol over the spare clothes box and set it on fire.

47. THE SCHOOL TOILET EXCUSE

The new school toilets just tried to kill me . . .

. . . the flush almost drowned me, the soap dispenser blinded me and the hand dryer made my hair look like this. I think I need to sit down for the next hour or so to recover.

48. THE ALLERGIES EXCUSE

Bad news Coach, I'm allergic to sport balls . . .

. . . so unless we all play with this imaginary basketball my doctor has given me I can not join in with today's lesson.

49. THE NEW T-SHIRT EXCUSE

Look Coach, I've bought a new t-shirt . . .

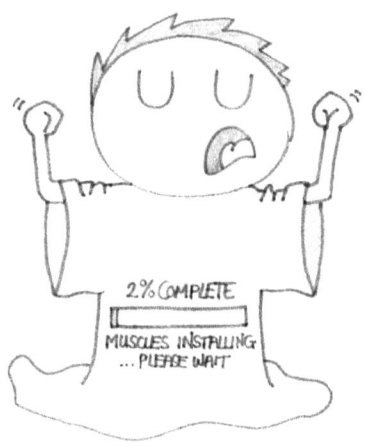

. . . all I have to do now is wait. I decided to go for the XXXL size to allow for plenty of space once the loading process is complete.

BONUS: DREAMS EXCUSE

I know you want me to run around the school field, but . . .

. . . I'm going back to bed. Why? Because I'm following your excellent advise - to never, ever give up on my *dreams*.

BONUS: HOGWARTS LETTER EXCUSE

I'm way too emotional to doing ANYTHING! . . .

. . . I have finally received a reply from Hogwarts. They have rejected my application.

BONUS: NEW WATCH EXCUSE

Great news, I've bought a brand new fitness watch . . .

. . . As the Gym Class teacher I know that your fitness watch must be telling you that you've got a chance. However, mine is telling me to just give up and go eat a brownie.

BONUS: DOUGHNUTS EXCUSE

Sir, I'm struggling to lose weight . . .

. . . What's my fitness and diet plan? I go for a run to the bakery and then eat an entire tray of doughnuts.

BONUS: ICE-CREAM EXCUSE

I believe you can pass Gym Class*.

*(by bribing the teacher with lots and lots of ice cream) . . .

James Warwood

BONUS: SWEATY EXCUSE

I can't run around the school field five times today . . .

. . . I've got a phobia for sweating. Sweat freaks me out! It's like smelly water that pours out from your armpits and dribbles all the way down to your socks. GROSS!!!

BONUS: JELLY LEGS EXCUSE

I would normally leap at the opportunely to run around the school field, but . . .

. . . I ran a 1,000,000k race yesterday. I won, of course. And now my legs have literally turned into jelly.

BONUS: OUT OF CHARGE EXCUSE

Do you have a fitness watch? . . .

. . . So do I, and because I'm so fit it's always out of charge. So, I'll be ready to take part in today's Gym Class lesson in four to six hours.

BONUS: SLUG EXCUSE

I've created a new fitness training routine inspired by slugs . . .

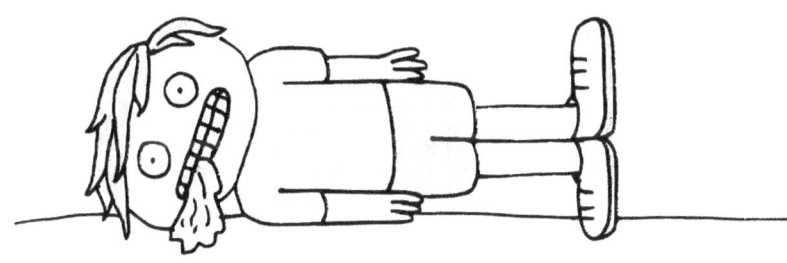

. . . Everyone and anyone can do it. It involves lying on the floor, eating lots of lettuce, more lying down and doing ABSOLUTELY nothing else.

BONUS: EXAM EXCUSE

LOOK! I passed the Ultimate Gym Class Written Exam . . .

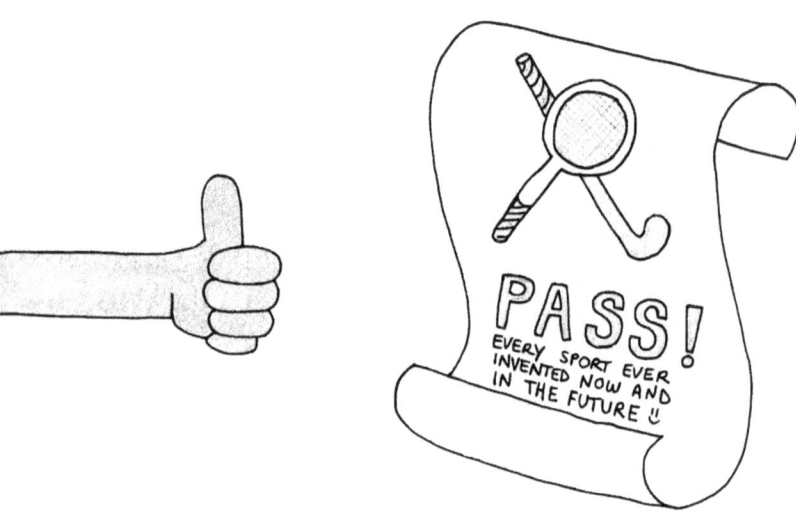

. . . I have nothing more to gain from Gym Class, so I won't be attending your lessons anymore and will be going to the School Library to 'study' instead.

BONUS: ARMPIT OF DOOM EXCUSE

Stand back! It's for your own safety . . .

. . . Why? Because my armpits smell like three-day-old baked beans. If I do Gym Class today, all the other students WILL pass out.

James Warwood

BONUS: ULTIMATE GYM EXAM EXCUSE

I'm taking the Ultimate Gym Class Exam . . .

. . . It's a written exam. So, instead of running around aimlessly in the freezing cold weather today as I'll be sitting in this lovely and warm room for the next two hours.

James Warwood is a writer and illustrator who lives on the borders of North Wales with his wife, two sons, and cactus (called Steve the Cactus).

He has a degree in Theology, which at the time seemed like a great idea, until he released he didn't want to become an RE Teacher. Instead, he writes laugh-out-loud middle grade fiction and non-fiction. He also fills them with his silly cartoons. He is the bestselling author of the EXCUSE ENCYCLOPEDIA and the TRUTH OR POOP SERIES.

James likes whiskey, squirrels, reading silly books, playing his bass guitar, and Greggs Sausage Rolls. He does not like losing at board games or having to writing about himself in the third person.

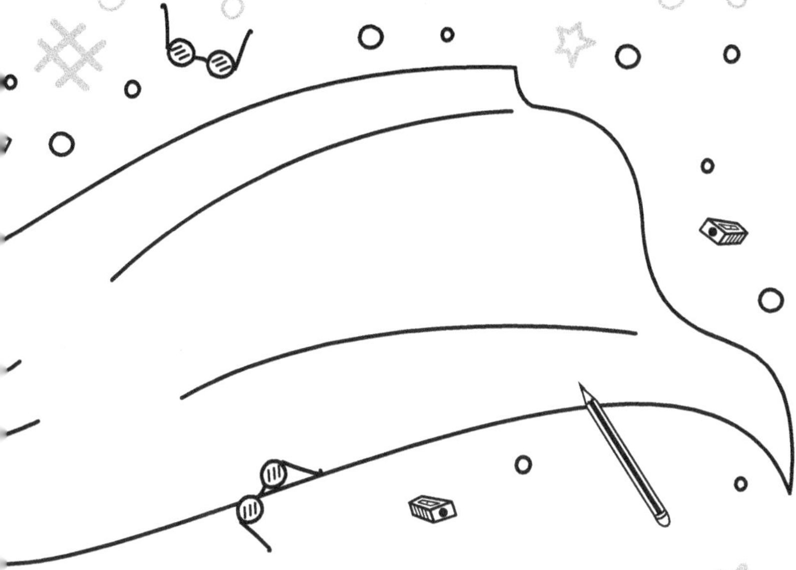

WHERE TO FIND JAMES ONLINE

Website: www.cjwarwood.com
Goodreads: James Warwood
Instagram: CJWarwood
Facebook: James Warwood

Want to join the
BOOKS & BISCUITS
CLUB?

Scan me to sign up
to the newsletter.

MIDDLE-GRADE STAND-ALONE FICTION

The Chef Who Cooked Up a Catastrophe
The Boy Who Stole One Million Socks
The Girl Who Vanquished the Dragon

TRUTH OR POOP SERIES

*True or false quiz books.
Learn something new and laugh as you do it!*

THE EXCUSE ENCYCLOPEDIA

11 more books to read!

GET THEM ALL IN THIS 12 IN 1 BUMPER EDITION!

820-page compendium of knowledge with 180 BONUS excuses

Scan me to activate your

25% DISCOUNT

www.ingramcontent.com/pod-product-compliance
Lightning Source LLC
Chambersburg PA
CBHW041314110526
44591CB00022B/2909